SASKIA GWINN   ADAM MING

I'M JOINING THE HERD

MEET OVER 50 ANIMALS WHO LIKE TO STICK TOGETHER

© 2025 Quarto Publishing plc
Text © 2025 Saskia Gwinn
Illustration © 2025 Adam Ming

Saskia Gwinn has asserted her right
to be identified as the author of this work.
Adam Ming has asserted his right
to be identified as the illustrator of this work.

Senior Designer: Sarah Chapman-Suire
Senior Commissioning Editor: Carly Madden
Editor: Amanda Askew
Consultant: Michael Bright
Creative Director: Malena Stojić
Associate Publisher: Rhiannon Findlay
Production Manager: Elizabeth Reardon

First published in 2025 by Happy Yak,
an imprint of The Quarto Group.
1 Triptych Place, London
SE1 9SH, United Kingdom.
T (0)20 7700 6700 F (0)20 7700 8066
EEA Representation, WTS Tax d.o.o.,
Žanova ulica 3, 4000 Kranj, Slovenia
www.quarto.com

No part of this publication may be reproduced, stored in a retrieval system, or transmitted in any form, or by any means, electrical, mechanical, photocopying, recording or otherwise, without the prior written permission of the publisher or a licence permitting restricted copying. In the United Kingdom, such licences are issued by the Copyright Licensing Agency, 5th Floor, Shackleton House, 4 Battle Bridge Lane, London SE1 2HX.

All rights reserved.

A catalogue record for this book is available from the British Library.

ISBN 978 0 7112 9558 2

Manufactured in Guangdong, China TT052025
9 8 7 6 5 4 3 2 1

CONTENTS

4 I'M JOINING THE HERD
Zebra

8 WE LIVE IN HERDS, TOO!
Caribou, musk ox, mountain goat, South American llama, impala, kangaroo

10 I'M ONE OF THE PACK
Grey wolf, grey lourie, flamingo, cheetah

12 I'M IN THE PARADE
African elephant

14 I'M CRUISING WITH MY CACKLE
Spotted hyena

16 I'M ROARING WITH MY PRIDE
Lion

18 I'M TEAM TOWER
Giraffe

20 I'M FLYING WITH MY FLOCK
Starling

For Arlo – S.G.

22 WE FLY IN FLOCKS, TOO!
Canada goose, scarlet macaw, swan, pelican

24 I'M COSY IN MY CAULDRON
Brown long-eared bat

26 WE'RE SNOOZING, TOO!
White tip reef shark, tadpole, chicken, meerkat

28 I'M FLOATING IN MY RAFT
Sea otter

30 I'M SINGING IN MY SCHOOL
Sperm whale, cricket, spring peeper frog, mouse

32 I'M PART OF A POD
Bottlenose dolphin

34 I'M SAFE IN MY SHOAL
Bluefin tuna

36 I'M TRAVELLING WITH MY TROOP
Yellow baboon

38 I'M AWESOME IN MY ARMY
Fire ant, sawfly caterpillar, army ant, swallowtail caterpillar, crazy ant, pine processionary caterpillar, monarch caterpillar

40 A KALEIDOSCOPE OF COLOUR
Monarch butterfly

42 SO WHO STICKS TOGETHER BEST?

46 WE STICK TOGETHER, TOO!
Oxpecker, rhino, cleaner wrasse, grey reef shark, drongo, meerkat

48 . . . WITH YOU!
Wildebeest, ostrich, eland, plover

I'M JOINING THE HERD

Now I'm three years old, I am BIG!

I can give hard kicks . . . POW!

I can be really LOUD!

BRAY!

And I'm fast when I'm escaping from lions!

I'm a *zebra* and I stay in my herd. My herd is the BEST. It makes me look strong to the rest of my world.

We help each other by nibbling hard-to-reach itches!

A group of zebras is called a HERD.

Although there are thousands of us, and we may all look the same, each set of stripes is . . .

WE LIVE IN HERDS, TOO!

I'm a **caribou**. Thousands of us rest, graze and travel together.

I'm a **musk ox**. We stand in a circle around the calves (babies) to protect them from predators.

I'm a **mountain goat**. We females live in herds of up to 20 goats. This protects our babies from danger, like steep cliffs or golden eagles.

Hummmm*

Humm**

I'm a **South American llama**. We hum to each other to show how we're feeling. Different hums can mean we're tired, anxious, content or curious.

*Quick! Something's coming!
**I'm tired.

I'm an *impala*. We help each other by leaping in the air together. This confuses an enemy who wants to gobble us up.

I'm a *kangaroo*. We pound our loud feet hard on the ground to tell the rest of the herd trouble is near.

BOOM BOOM BOOM!

Hummmm***

Zebra, over here!

***LLAMAS work BETTER when we stick together!

I'M ONE OF THE PACK

I'm a **grey wolf**. We take it in turns to catch dinner, so our pups have plenty to eat.

A group of wolves is called a PACK.

When the pups are older, we teach them how to hunt.

The pups play and pounce with friends in the pack.

When you hear an . . .

AR-OOOOO!

. . . it's a wolf's call. It means 'Come here – something's been caught'. Dinnertime!

WOLVES work BETTER when we stick together!

Er, I don't fancy that . . .

I'M IN THE PARADE

I'm an **African elephant**. I live in a group that's led by my mum.

Milk time!

In our group there are mums, babies and other females. And it's GREAT!

If I'm hungry, I'm fed and if I'm stuck, I'm helped out.

PUSSH!!

If I'm scared, there's always a friend nearby.

It'll be okay.

I'M ROARING WITH MY PRIDE

I'm a **lion** and we roar together to mark our territory. Our roar is so LOUD, it can be heard from miles away!

ROOOOOOAAAAR!!!

We clean each other...

LICK!

...and look after all of the cubs together.

A group of lions is called a PRIDE.

I'M TEAM TOWER!

I'm a *giraffe* and I'm as tall as can be! We stick together so lions don't come close. But if they do, they get a colossal, karate-style KICK!

Hi-YA! Be off with you!

We hang out with our family and friends. We share food such as thorny acacia trees.

We females are eating from the lower branches.

We males are nibbling from the treetops.

There are enough leaves for everyone!

I'M FLYING WITH MY FLOCK

I'm a *starling*. Just before dusk when the sun's almost set, thousands of starlings gather in the sky to . . .

TWIST . . .

SWOOP . . .

and FLY!

We stay in our group by following a starling that's flying close by.

A group of starlings is called a FLOCK or a MURMURATION.

This way! Follow her!

That way! Follow him!

I can't keep up!

Of course you can't. You're a zebra.

WE FLY IN FLOCKS, TOO!

I'm a **Canada goose**. My flock flies together in a V-shape.

My flock is called a GAGGLE.

I'm a **scarlet macaw**. We live together in rainforests in large, noisy flocks.

My flock is called a COMPANY.

I'm a **swan**. We gather in our flock to feed and travel.

My flock is called a FLEET.

I'M COSY IN MY CAULDRON

I'm a **brown long-eared bat** and we hunt through the night, feasting on bugs by swooping down to . . .

. . . BITE!

In summer, we roost in buildings or barns with the bats we know best.

WE'RE SNOOZING, TOO!

I'm a *white tip reef shark*. We gather together in a pile to snooze – though our eyes stay open wide!

A group of sharks is called a SHIVER.

"We can see you!"

"Eek!"

I'm a *tadpole*. I'm one of 400 having a little nap. There's safety in numbers!

A group of tadpoles is called a KNOT.

"Oh no!"

I'm a **chicken**. At night we snooze close together on a roost up high to keep warm and feel safe.

A group of chickens is called a BROOD.

I'm a **meerkat**. We snuggle up together in our tunnel.

A group of meerkats is called a MOB.

Ahhh, cute.

WE all work BETTER when we stick together!

Did someone say snuggle?

I'M SINGING IN MY SCHOOL

I'm a **sperm whale**. We gather in groups not far from the surface, then sleep whilst floating upright!

A group of sperm whales is called a POD.

When we're awake we sing to each other. We can tell from miles away if a whale is in our group by their whale song.

Time for a song . . .

CLICK CLICK CLICK. CLICKETY CLICK CLICKKKK!

SPERM WHALES work BETTER when we stick together!

WE ALL SING, TOO!

I'm a male **cricket** and I sing to attract a female.

Chirp chirp chirp!

I'm a **spring peeper frog** and I 'peep' to show that spring is here.

Peep peep peep!

Don't you croak?

Peep! NOPE.

I'm a **mouse**. I squeak when I'm hungry, scared, injured, want to be friends or . . . for anything else.

Squeak squeak SQUEEEAK.

Hey, Zebra! This way . . .

I'M SAFE IN MY SHOAL

I'm a **bluefin tuna** and we follow three rules:

1. Stay close to each other.
2. Keep on swimming.
3. Don't EVER stray from the group.

UH-OH, ORCA!

GULP.

A group of tuna is called a SCHOOL.

Oh no! I forgot the rules!

I'M AWESOME IN MY ARMY

I'm a *fire ant*. We literally stick together! We join our bodies to build bridges between branches, leaves and brooks.

A group of ants is called an ARMY or a COLONY.

I'm a *sawfly caterpillar*. We travel by rolling over each other to create a conveyor belt! It makes us super fast!

A group of caterpillars is called an ARMY or a SWARM.

Well, I'm an *army ant* and WE march in a line to find our way back to our nest.

Well, I'm a *swallowtail caterpillar* and WE leave a stinky smell to frighten away predators.

Well, I'm a **crazy ant** and WE carry giant pieces of food up to 50 times our own body weight.

Hey, watch where you put your nose!

Well, I'm a **pine processionary caterpillar** and . . . WE can walk upright.

Well, we **fire ants** can ALSO make rafts!

WOOHOO!

Well, I'm a **monarch caterpillar** and, like all caterpillars, WE eat and eat and EAT, before we each turn into a chrysalis. But the big finish is . . .

SO WHO STICKS TOGETHER *BEST?*

Zebra thinks very carefully about this and decides...

We ALL work better when we stick together!

Hyenas, as well as *lions* and *wolves*, work better when they hunt together.

Shall we be friends?

Bottlenose dolphins work better when they trick fish together.

Bats, reef sharks, tadpoles, sea otters, chickens and *meerkats* work better when they snooze together.

Baboons work better when they pick ticks together.

Caribou, musk oxen, impalas and *kangaroos* work better when they live together.

This is lovely!

Tuna work better when they swim close together.

Caterpillars, ants and monarch butterflies work better when they move around together.

Starlings, geese, swans, macaws and pelicans work better when they fly together.

Elephants work better when they travel together.

And zebras work better when they stay strong together.

But wait! Zebra! You forgot about us . . .

WE STICK TOGETHER, TOO!

We work together, even though we are different.

I'm a *rhino*. I provide a tasty treat of parasites for an oxpecker.

I'm an *oxpecker*. I pick off parasites from a rhino's thick skin.